GREAT RIVER REGIONAL LIBRARY

Please Do Not Color

W9-BAL-007

SPORTS
HIDDEN PICTURES

Selected by Jody Taylor

Boyds Mills Press

3379351

GREAT RIVER REGIONAL LIBRARY

Copyright © 1993 by Boyds Mills Press
All rights reserved

Published by Bell Books
Boyds Mills Press, Inc.
A Highlights Company
815 Church Street
Honesdale, Pennsylvania 18431
Printed in the United States of America

Publisher Cataloging-in-Publication Data
Main entry under title.
    Sports hidden pictures / selected by Jody Taylor.—1st ed.
[32]p. : ill. ; cm.
Summary: Various objects are hidden in illustrations of sports scenes.
ISBN 1-56397-255-7
1. Puzzles—Juvenile literature. [1. Picture puzzles.] I. Taylor, Jody.
II. Title.
793.73—dc20   1993   CIP
Library of Congress Catalog Card Number: 92-76173

First edition, 1993
Book designed by Tim Gillner
The text of this book is set in 10-point Clarendon Light.
Distributed by St. Martin's Press

10 9 8 7 6 5 4 3 2 1

Volleyball Action

Can Ryan spike the ball over the net to win the game? And can you find the hidden objects in this picture? Look for a pitcher, snow shovel, ladder, sneaker, bird, pig, book, cat, sink plunger, hammer, and a rabbit.

The Lizards' Foot Race

It looks as if Number 7 will take home the winner's cup. As the rest of the lizards cross the finish line, look for these hidden objects: a boot, turtle, hanger, wristwatch, hockey stick, hat, fish, hammer, light bulb, necktie, bowl, ladle, bone, and a baby's bottle.

Go, Tigers!

Basketball games are always challenging, but finding these hidden objects is, too. Can you find a cat, ladle, sewing needle, football, harmonica, chicken, saltshaker, pea pod, bottle, flower pot, acorn, bowling pin, iron, sea gull, pitcher, and a spool of thread?

Surf's Up!

While the dogs enjoy a day of sand, surf, and fun, try to find the hidden book, artist's paintbrush, ice-cream pop, bone, Santa's hat, apple core, bird, mouse, Christmas tree ornament, wishbone, fork, pencil, spoon, and the penguin.

Broom Hockey Champs

For wintertime fun, nothing beats a fast-paced game of broom hockey. In this picture find the squirrel, comb, mug, golf club, postage stamp, goldfish, bird, rose, artist's paintbrush, sailboat, heart, pencil, spool of thread, and the dog's head.

Windsurfing Canines

Oops! One of the windsurfing dogs may be going for an unexpected swim. In the meantime, look for thirteen hidden objects: a hammer, ice-cream cone, kite, top hat, goose, pennant, frog, bugle, sailboat, banana, fish, beaver, and a baseball bat.

Who's Got the Ball?

The professional football players in this early 1900s scene are battling for possession of the ball, but young Christopher scores the touchdown to end the game. Help him find the cat, hairbrush, mouse, doughnut, slice of cheese, mug, lamb, telephone receiver, ax, banana, ice-cream cone, hammer, envelope, and the elephant's head.

Skating Bears

Out of the way! The Bear family is skating down Main Street. They're moving too fast to see the hidden objects. See if you can find the spaceship, carrot, toothbrush, screwdriver, orange slice, baseball, mushroom, sink plunger, spatula, balloon, artist's paintbrush, telephone receiver, teacup, stopwatch, high-heeled shoe, and the tape dispenser.

Kayaking Duo

As Scott and his dad begin to paddle carefully through the white water part of their downriver journey, try to locate eighteen objects hidden all around them. Look for a seashell, bird, pencil, fish, arrowhead, penguin, balloon, mouse, rabbit, shark, bat, artist's paintbrush, frog, bottle, saw, turtle, wasp, and a heron.

On the Offensive

Mindy shows some fancy footwork and leads her team to victory. You can score big if you can find these hidden objects: a button, snail, bedroom slipper, fish, cupcake, pliers, ice-cream cone, turkey leg, saltshaker, crescent moon, ladder, canteen, bird, flashlight, nutcracker, and a high-heeled shoe.

Downhill Fun

It's a perfect day for skiing, and Kristen and the other members of the ski club are having too much fun to notice some hidden objects. Can you find a turtle, heart, feather, bird, orange slice, fish, canoe, baseball, dog, cupcake, bat, bowl, flower, toothbrush, and a crescent moon?

Cross-Country Bike Race

It's a close race as the dogs round the final bend. In this picture find the duck, eagle's head, shark, hammer, stocking cap, alligator, wasp, otter, penguin, butterfly, feather, bird, and the elf's head.

Softball Victory

The team is so excited about Dara's winning run that they don't notice any hidden objects. Do you see a slice of pie, artist's paintbrush, bone, sheep, three arrows, earthworm, starfish, beet, mushroom, piece of cheese, opossum, and a slice of toast?

Spring Practice

The kangaroo rats are practicing hard for their first baseball game. In the meantime, can you spot the hidden saw, creamer, frog, bottle, feather, shoe, key, goose, open book, paper clip, hot dog, spoon, and the ear of corn?

The Marathon

As the children race, can you find the seventeen objects hiding in this picture? Look for a candle, book, mouse, garden hoe, apple core, baton, mug, bottle, fishhook, toothbrush, hammer, cat, earthworm, horseshoe, bowl, pencil, and a slice of bread.

Underwater Adventure

Finally the divers have found the long-lost sunken ship and its treasure. Will they also find the hidden mouse, key, envelope, baseball bat, squirrel, apple, bee, toothbrush, crescent moon, snail, kite, baseball, two birds, and the letter **H**?

Soccer Fun

Soccer is a fast-paced game. How quickly can you locate fifteen hidden objects in this picture? Look for a hammer, sailboat, bottle, parrot, seal, leaf, nail, turtle, spoon, gerbil, saw, chick, fish, slice of pie, and a high-heeled shoe.

Ice Hockey Excitement

While Jake sends the puck sailing past the other team's goaltender, try to find ten hidden objects: a shark, rabbit, bird, butterfly, mouse, squirrel, lion, bear, armadillo, and a dog's head.

Rollerblade Kids

Jonathan watches admiringly as Mark and Sarah fly by on their new rollerblades. Did you notice sixteen objects hidden throughout this picture? Look for a pear, table, bird, playing card, man's head, spoon, fish, teacup, lemon slice, padlock, duck, boot, banana, artist's paintbrush, earthworm, and a hockey stick.

After-School Scrimmage

As Amy and the twins watch the football team practice for its first game of the season, see if you can find a mouse, trowel, football player, two witches, ear of corn, fountain pen, football, cat, and a witch's broom.

The Golf Tournament

What can the forest animals do on a perfect spring day? Play their own version of miniature golf, of course. Meanwhile, try to find fifteen objects hidden in this picture: a pumpkin, bird, pliers, snake, boot, key, fish, toothbrush, ring, airplane, teacup, sailboat, watering can, pencil, and a mushroom.

Skateboarding Trio

Look out! Jen, Paul, and Jason are having so much fun skateboarding they don't even notice all the hidden objects on and around them. Can you find the parrot, candle, artist's paintbrush, hammer, spoon, golf club, rabbit, slice of pie, toothbrush, eyeglasses, hobbyhorse, and the broom?

Final Minutes of Play

Will Valerie get past the other team's defense to make the winning basket? And will you be able to spot all the hidden objects in this picture? Look for the bowling pin, fish, cat, ring, eyeglasses, teacup, toothbrush, carrot, bird, mouse, penguin, cupcake, goose, and the flute.

On the Trail

These kittens are trying to earn scouting badges in hiking and trail finding. As they stop to check map and compass, look for a mouse, sewing needle, goldfish, paper clip, bird, rabbit's head, crab, snail, teacup, acorn, number 7, apple, turtle, carrot, and a bee.

Ski Race

Who will be the first skier to reach the bottom of the slope? As the racers dash by, find the comb, bandage, cane, pencil, open book, baby's head, rabbit, iron, dog's head, ball-point pen, artist's paintbrush, and the kite.

Mountain-Climbing Friends

The bear needs some help from his animal friends to get up the cliff. You can help them by finding the fish, castle, baton, boomerang, wishbone, caboose, life preserver, football helmet, dust mop, bee, pineapple, bow, and the peanut.

ANSWERS

Cover: twelve baseballs

3: pitcher, snow shovel, ladder, sneaker, bird, pig, book, cat, sink plunger, hammer, rabbit

4: boot, turtle, hanger, wristwatch, hockey stick, hat, fish, hammer, light bulb, necktie, bowl, ladle, bone, baby's bottle

5: cat, ladle, sewing needle, football, harmonica, chicken, saltshaker, pea pod, bottle, flower pot, acorn, bowling pin, iron, sea gull, pitcher, spool of thread

6: hidden book, artist's paintbrush, ice-cream pop, bone, Santa's hat, apple core, bird, mouse, Christmas tree ornament, wishbone, fork, pencil, spoon, penguin

7: squirrel, comb, mug, golf club, postage stamp, goldfish, bird, rose, artist's paintbrush, sailboat, heart, pencil, spool of thread, dog's head

8: hammer, ice-cream cone, kite, top hat, goose, pennant, frog, bugle, sailboat, banana, fish, beaver, baseball bat

9: cat, hairbrush, mouse, doughnut, slice of cheese, mug, lamb, telephone receiver, ax, banana, ice-cream cone, hammer, envelope, elephant's head

10: spaceship, carrot, toothbrush, screwdriver, orange slice, baseball, mushroom, sink plunger, spatula, balloon, artist's paintbrush, telephone receiver, teacup, stopwatch, high-heeled shoe, tape dispenser

11: seashell, bird, pencil, fish, arrowhead, penguin, balloon, mouse, rabbit, shark, bat, artist's paintbrush, frog, bottle, saw, turtle, wasp, heron

12: button, snail, bedroom slipper, fish, cupcake, pliers, ice-cream cone, turkey leg, saltshaker, crescent moon, ladder, canteen, bird, flashlight, nutcracker, high-heeled shoe

13: turtle, heart, feather, bird, orange slice, fish, canoe, baseball, dog, cupcake, bat, bowl, flower, toothbrush, crescent moon

14: duck, eagle's head, shark, hammer, stocking cap, alligator, wasp, otter, penguin, butterfly, feather, bird, elf's head

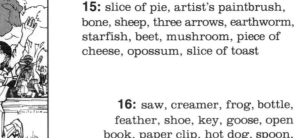

15: slice of pie, artist's paintbrush, bone, sheep, three arrows, earthworm, starfish, beet, mushroom, piece of cheese, opossum, slice of toast

16: saw, creamer, frog, bottle, feather, shoe, key, goose, open book, paper clip, hot dog, spoon, ear of corn

17: candle, book, mouse, garden hoe, apple core, baton, mug, bottle, fishhook, toothbrush, hammer, cat, earthworm, horseshoe, bowl, pencil, slice of bread

18: mouse, key, envelope, baseball bat, squirrel, apple, bee, toothbrush, crescent moon, snail, kite, baseball, two birds, letter **H**

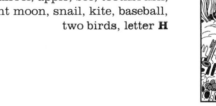

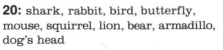

19: hammer, sailboat, bottle, parrot, seal, leaf, nail, turtle, spoon, gerbil, saw, chick, fish, slice of pie, high-heeled shoe

20: shark, rabbit, bird, butterfly, mouse, squirrel, lion, bear, armadillo, dog's head

21: pear, table, bird, playing card, man's head, spoon, fish, teacup, lemon slice, padlock, duck, boot, banana, artist's paintbrush, earthworm, hockey stick

22: mouse, trowel, football player, two witches, ear of corn, fountain pen, football, cat, witch's broom

23: pumpkin, bird, pliers, snake, boot, key, fish, toothbrush, ring, airplane, teacup, sailboat, watering can, pencil, mushroom

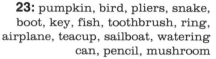

24: parrot, candle, artist's paintbrush, hammer, spoon, golf club, rabbit, slice of pie, toothbrush, eyeglasses, hobbyhorse, broom

25: bowling pin, fish, cat, ring, eyeglasses, teacup, toothbrush, carrot, bird, mouse, penguin, cupcake, goose, flute

26: mouse, sewing needle, goldfish, paper clip, bird, rabbit's head, crab, snail, teacup, acorn, number 7, apple, turtle, carrot, bee

27: comb, bandage, cane, pencil, open book, baby's head, rabbit, iron, dog's head, ball-point pen, artist's paintbrush, kite

28: fish, castle, baton, boomerang, wishbone, caboose, life preserver, football helmet, dust mop, bee, pineapple, bow, peanut

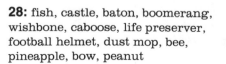